THE EXPERIMENTS

[a legend in pictures & words]

THE EXPERIMENTS

[a legend in pictures & words]

RACHEL MAY

DUSIE

Excerpts from this collection were first published in the following literary journals: An image was featured on the cover of *Michigan Quarterly Review* Winter 2014, in addition to a series of images and text, "Remember," published within that issue. A series of shorts & images under the title "Quiet" was published in *1913: A Journal of Forms*; "Remember: A Legend in Words and Pictures" was published in *New Delta Review*, Spring 2013. "Avery" was published in *The Literary Review*, Fall 2012. A series of shorts and images under the title "The Vermont Studio Center Experiments" was published in *Word/for Word*, Spring 2012. A series of shorts under the title "Good" was published in *Sleepingfish*, Winter 2009–2010. "Bee & Grim" was published in *Michigan Quarterly Review*, Winter/Spring 2011. "The Gold Dust Room" was published in *Green Mountains Review*, Spring 2010.

Cover art: *Sea Monster*, Rachel May

Layout and Book Design by DUSIE
dusie.org | Kingston, RI

First printing, Rachel May, 2015

ISBN-13: 9780692462966

Contents

"We might begin with Anne Bradstreet's famous line: 'I am obnoxious to each carping tongue / Who says my hand a needle better fits.' That sentence establishes a creative tension between pens and needles, hands and tongues, written and nonwritten forms of female expression, inviting us not only to take oral traditions and material sources more seriously…but also to examine the roots of the written documents we take so much for granted."

- Laurel Thatcher Ulrich, "Of Pens & Needles"

"'Has the pen or pencil dipped so deep in the blood of the human race as the needle?' asked the writer Olive Schreiner. The answer is, quite simply, no. The art of embroidery has been the means of educating women into the feminine ideal, and of proving that they have attained it, but it has also provided a weapon of resistance to the constraints of femininity."

- Rozsika Parker, *The Subversive Stitch*

Sew, Knot, Weave

The people who had had it done could no longer remember things—their wives' names, their children's birth dates, to whom the animal in the living room belonged (*The dog*, says the child in the orange striped shirt, *is Bendo, and he is ours*). They had been warned that this might happen, in the experiments, but it was a way to get out of the misery, and they were desperate, and they tried. So much of it was like it's always been—the jaw clamped shut, the current running through the body—but now, said the people who'd done it, there was less pain, and something spiritual—visions, a gentleness in the mind, after. Gradients of white, the people kept repeating. Gray? the others would ask. No, it was insisted, shades of white. One woman forgot her whole family, and now she felt alone, and things were worse. A man bellowed on and on about how it hadn't *fucking* worked and he couldn't drink and he'd given up his fucking marriage, after all this. But a younger man said it was a miracle, and he was paying off his house with the antique cars he'd sold off, and he loved his children when he looked at them now. For so long, he hadn't felt anything for them. The woman who was about to get

married retrained her brain to remember things about her fiancée —
where they'd met (Ontario), what he liked to eat best (fried chicken
fingers with barbeque sauce, spicy), when they'd be married (two
months, on a beach with humped rocks in Oregon). She felt delight.
She was not alone. When it worked, it really worked, and that was
worth the effort, the loss of memory, the body seething with electric-
ity, little sparks flying from the fingertips and the earlobes and the
toes, spinning into air like the body's forgotten stars.

✳

Bury it, burn it, solder it together, wear it for a while and then leave it in its shape, submerge it in water, leave it on the dirt, in the sun, in the wind, in the rain, let the dew fall on it in the morning from the rooftop; if you don't like it as it is, wash it and it will turn into something else. Or you can felt it, sew it, embroider it, mold it, sculpt it, shape it, heal it, unweave it, knot it, weave it back together in another shape, paint it, set it on ice and let it melt into itself. Set it by a river, set it in the dirt, put animal bones in it, hair in it, leaves in it, keep it as a keepsake on your wall, ask other people to perform it, ask other people to hold it or caress it or treat it like a mother or a child, and don't interfere when they treat it like a lover, because it's in our nature to change the shape of things, to turn every bit of earth and material into memory, or salve.

*

When dolls have sex on the screen, and the hands hold the dolls, I feel uncomfortable. One is just a ghost doll, and one is a real doll. The ghost doll has an open mouth. The ghost doll is starving for something. The real doll has brown hair, and climbs on the ghost doll, which is what happens in real life sometimes, the crawling yearning of it—which isn't always pretty. But sometimes, like at the end of the doll serenade, it is so good.

*

She watched all the videos of herself when she was small, when she
was learning words and forgetting them. She does not remember this
time, and that is probably for the best. It was a very painful time.
The man would tell her stories, stories about Bobo the bunny who
was black and white and liked to eat lettuce and carrots. That was
the whole story, and he would say, What was the bunny's name?
And she was four, and she would look at the man, and watch his face
for clues, and rub at her lips and pull at her chin, and he would say,
No, don't do that. And she would remember that she was not supposed to rub at her lips or pull at her chin, and put her hand down.
And he would say, What was the bunny's name? And she would
look at the man for clues, and start to raise her hand, and he would
say, Nope, and she would put her hand down. And she would watch
his lips. And he would say, B, b, b. And she would say, B, b, b. And
he would say, What was the bunny's name? And she would say, The
bunny's name. And he would say, B, b, b. And she would squinch
up her face and squint her eyes, and put up her hand and lower
her hand, and he would say, What was the bunny's name? And he
would say, Bobo. And she would say, Bobo! Very excited, and he
would say, Yes! Bobo! And she would say, Bobo! And she knew
that she had gotten it right. He would say, What was the bunny's
name? And she would say, The bunny's name. He would say, B, b,
b. And she would say, B, b, b. He would say, Bobo! And she would
say Bobo! And he would say, Very good! And touch her hand or her
head or her arm and make her feel very proud. He would say, What
did the bunny eat? And she would look at him, and touch her lips,
and pull at her chin, and he'd say, Nope! And she'd put her hands
down. And he would say it again, and again, and what color was the
bunny, again, and again, and it was so difficult and so painful, and
she knew, as an adult, that her mother was sitting in another room,
crying. Her mother did not believe she'd ever get better. Luckily,
she surprised her mother. So, years later, when she was fourteen

and did not remember this time, the man who had taught her the words came back and said to her mother that he wanted to make a documentary about her journey, and her mother said, I never told her she used to be wordless, and he said, Think about it, then. And he left. So her mother thought. If she did not tell her daughter, what would her daughter lose? Her history, herself. She knew. So she told her daughter, and she watched the videos with her daughter, and her daughter wept and said, I always knew somehow I was different. And her mother said, But look how strong. They had gone to great lengths to cover this past. They had moved away from their old town, from the old school. The little girl was known as someone who had never had these problems. She had a brand new life, with no associations with that past. But now, at last, she knew. She knew her whole history, and she thanked her mother, and began to speak about her history. And in the speaking, she began to see herself, and understand herself. She goes back sometimes and looks at the old videos, though, and sees how hard she was trying then, and how difficult it was, how painful, and she gets goose bumps all up and down her arms and legs, as if her body can't help remembering what her mind protects her from.

✳

This woman smeared cupcake frosting on her face because it was good for her skin. This woman's name was Bill, which was a strange name for a woman but no one ever questioned it because they liked her. She was tall and dark-haired, and she had buck teeth. Sometimes, the new ones, they would make fun of her buck teeth behind her back, and the old ones would say, No, no, don't do that to Bill; Bill is good. And they would stop.

Why did Bill smear frosting on her face? said the new ones, and the old ones said, Why do you wear shoes? And the new ones laughed, and looked down at their feet, and noticed that their shoes were gone. The rules were different in this world, they were beginning to see. They were beginning to feel uncomfortable.

Well, said the old ones, We have only grass here; why would you need shoes?

But what about the craters? said the new ones, and the old ones said, We avoid the craters. That's the only way.
The new ones looked at each other, and looked at the old ones, and looked at Bill, who sat in the corner smearing cupcake frosting all over her face—it was all over her hands now, too, and in big fat pink and white smudges on the table—and they said, We come from a place that does not endorse avoidance.

The old ones said, Why the hell not? Look how it works for us! The new ones said, We've learned some things that you might not know.

Well, said the old ones, and they crossed their arms and looked at each other and wondered who these ostentatious fools could be.

One of the grayest old ones stepped forward and said, Why don't you tell us about your practices, then? Why don't you tell us about how you don't avoid? What is your land like—all fairy dust and fine sand?

The new ones sensed their attitude and tried not to react. They were practicing openness. They laughed. They opened their arms and gestured and leaned forward, toward the old ones. Actually, they said, we come from a place with mountains and volcanoes and beaches. But the beaches are rocky, not sandy. And there are pine trees along the shore, and snow-crested peaks, and, inland, we get droughts all summer long. Cacti and sage brush grow.

The old ones raised their eyebrows, turned down their lips, and shrugged. Eh, said one. We've seen worse.

One of the new ones said, Oh? But look at all this grass.

The old ones said, We planted this grass a long time ago. We cultivated it, and changed our climate for it, and worked very hard to make sure it stays lush and green and soft under our feet.

The news ones looked at each other now, wondering if this could be true. Changed your climate? they said. The old ones nodded, looked back to Bill, and leaned in, stage-whisper. We built a sun shield, so we don't get too much. We control the hours of the day, how much in which season. We keep the temperature between seventy-five and eighty, and we let it rain more in the winter.

But, said the new ones, what did it used to look like here?

The old ones said, Rocky, and dry, and windy. Too many dust storms. Too much drought. Too many sharp pieces to walk upon.

The new ones frowned and looked down at their bare feet, at the green grass, and imagined what was underneath: the real bumpy earth, all covered up, as if shamed. Hm, they said.

The old ones said, We had no choice! Our feet were all cracked and sore, our eyes were red, our bodies were parched and tired. What could we do?

The new ones said, We made clothes for ourselves. We made shoes. We made goggles and lip balm and gloves. Sunscreen. Hats. The old ones looked at each other, arms crossed. Well, they said, we chose another way.

Let us see the craters, said the new ones.

The old ones said they wouldn't go back there; they just pointed the way: west. Sunset is at seven every day, they said, Be back by then.

All right, said the new ones, and off they went, barefoot.

They got to the craters by five, an hour later, after several wrong turns over the grassy land.

When they found their own pressed-in-prints in the grass, they realized they'd gone in a circle. One of them took a compass from his pocket. Don't let the old ones see *that*, said another of the new ones, *a tool! Oh no!* They laughed. They kept walking.

At last, they found the craters, and they saw that they were wide and deep and full of some sort of smoke. The craters sometimes coughed up water, and then pulled the water back in, slurping, and the water was tinged yellow and smelled of sulfur. In the distance, there was one geyser, which sent up a stream of water every seven minutes, twenty feet into the air. Then the water rested in a pool around the geyser, and slowly sank back into the earth.

One of the new ones gasped and said, It looks like home, and another said, Yes.

They decided to sit beside the craters, on the dirt, not the grass, and to rest their heads on their knees, and watch. They were homesick. They didn't like the sight of all that green, homogenous, unnatural. They missed their unsightly home.

They sat through dinner. They sat through sunset. They sat through the whole night, with the stars coming up, and the geyser sending up its shoot every seven minutes. Right on time. And the sound of water splashing out, and of the craters taking the water back in. They all dozed off. They fell against each other, sleeping.

They woke up at sunrise. In the morning, they sat and watched a while longer, and then began to stand and stretch and say, I'm hungry, and talk about what to do.

Should we walk back? they said.

What's the point? said one.

And another said, I like to watch Bill; Bill's strange and funny.

The others said, That's not a good enough reason to return.

Well, said one, it's obvious, isn't it? We could start a revolution.

The others looked at each other and nodded and shrugged and said, Easy enough. Why not?

So they put on some bandanas, tied around their biceps, and they took out their guitars, and they grew their hair long and kept their feet bare and said, Now we are hippies. And they went back, in pursuit of the natural earth, a fight on their fingertips.

When the old ones saw the new ones coming, they remembered, and knew what to expect. They ushered all the other old ones into the big gray building at the edge of nothing—in the midst of all that green—and said it was a climate emergency, to stay inside, please, until it's safe. One of the old ones stood at the door, and waited until all the old ones were inside, and then bolted the door shut, closing themselves in. The new ones stood outside the door. They held hands. They sang kumbaya.

Then one of them said, I think we need more to this revolution, this is all too superficial, this is just an idea of a revolution.

So one of them took out the guitar and sang about the homogenous green grass and the real weather they were missing and the unnaturalness of this place, the environment they'd covered and ruined. They sang about the geysers and the sulfur smell and the sound of water. They sang about rain and wind and sun and dust. They sang about the way the weather changed, and the things people had to say about it—how a week of rain could string people together, could unite them in their mild misery, how when the sun came out after that week of rain, everyone would smile and laugh together, and walk into the sun with their faces turned up, like flowers.

The old ones inside heard all of this, because the old ones had forgotten to soundproof the building (never expecting a revolution, any discontent, any unhappiness in the face of all that green and sunshine), and one of the old ones, upon hearing the word geyser, remembered driving through Yellowstone Park as a child, and seeing Old Faithful, his face pressed up against the station wagon window, and he was filled with such nostalgia and such longing, that he pushed himself through the crowd, and walked into the sunshine, and—even though the other old ones screamed and beckoned for him to come back—he joined the singing hippies, and wooed the rest.

Eventually, all their memories came back to them, memories of childhoods in the woods, by the sea, on rainy camping trips, in thunderstorms, in the sunshine at a barbeque, in the wind on a mountain, shivering, exhilarated. These memories rose above the crowd and drifted out into the world, and they all pressed forward, into the air and onto the green grass and under the sunshine. They held hands and they sang, and sang, and sang, feeling not even a little bit self-conscious.

Then, the few old ones remaining, the ones who had hatched

the environmental plan and built the shield and changed the weather, they said, You don't remember the pain! This is what you don't remember. All you're remembering now is the good. Remember how much it hurt? Remember how much your bodies ached and your heads were tired and your energy was sapped by all that weather? Remember how you hated the snow in February, and got frostbite and lost one of your toes? Remember how the wind chapped your cheeks? And the sun burned your skin? And your feet were calloused and bleeding? You don't remember all of that. We have saved you from it. Look at this green grass! Look how smooth and easy it is! Look how lucky you are! And the new ones looked around, and the old ones looked around, and all across this land, all the way to the horizon, there was green, and it was true: It was easy.

But now they heard the sounds underneath the grass—the rivers running, which would flood when they were cut loose. The craters and the geysers and the dry earth in the summertime. They heard this and they smelled it, and they couldn't stand the sight of the grass anymore. Not for one second more.

One of them cried and said, We're ready for pain. It will bring surprises. It won't all be pain. Remember?

The old ones, the ones who were afraid, looked at each other and sat down, and cried. They threw up their hands.

They said, You're going to do it, anyway, aren't you?

The new ones said, Yes.

The old ones said, All our work?

The new ones said, We're sorry.

They all knelt down, and began to pull back the grass.

It came up like sod, like it had never really taken root, had known it did not belong, should not be used as a shield. Grass grows where it's natural to grow—on hills, in dunes, in little woodsy clearings—and is otherwise never quite at ease, always needing so much coddling and encouragement to stay put. So it was easy to pull up the grass, and to reveal everything that was underneath. And to put up ladders and peel back the shield, and let the sun and the moon and the clouds—the real ones, not the fake ones—shine down.

Bill stopped smearing frosting on her face and helped to pull back the grass, and didn't care about trying to make her skin perfect anymore, because she had more important things to tend to now.

Perfection, she said, is irrelevant.

They found the trees wrapped up in background colors, and

unwrapped them, and they yanked down all those fake stars and let the real ones free.

After all this work, three days of work, the new ones were tired, and went out for beers, and the old ones, still sitting on their last remaining little patch of grass, just big enough for their bottoms, looked up and around. It was a cloudy day. A small breeze. The humidity was much too high. They wished to lower it. They were so uncomfortable just sitting there, and they itched to do something to make it better, to re-cover the earth, to cover the sky, to make everything easier. The river was about to overflow, they saw, and it would flood the dirt and make mud! The mess of it! They wanted to fix it. But they couldn't, now. It had all been undone. So they sat and they sat and they sat, through their discomfort and through the itch and through the fear that they would all burn or melt or get blown away. They cried. They screamed. They were miserable. They hated it, all this discomfort, and they cursed the new people, who were off getting drunk, and they cursed the world for being so disorderly and unpredictable, and they cursed themselves for getting into this mess, and they yelled at each other for not being able to stop the undoing, the revolution—but they did not move. Not once. They kept their arms around their knees, as if to hold themselves together.

They realized, after seven hours of wailing and crying and discomfort, that they were still alive. They had not died. They looked at each other, amazed. They looked at the world, all laid bare, and they were amazed at that, too. At all the different ways the landscape looked. At the rises and the dips and the rocks and the rivers and the streams, and now that it was nighttime, at the way the moon reflected in the streams in a silver color they hadn't seen in years, and the stars, and the deep blue color of the sky.

Please don't leave me.
Don't give up on me.

＊

31

Once, I was a peanut-butter truck, and I smelled good inside. Everyone wanted to drive me because I reminded them of things they liked: moments when their mothers were nice, the sound of naptime, bananas, sticky tongues that made words all wrong. And laughing. They liked to laugh. When I was a peanut-butter truck, I think I made a lot of friends, but I could never tell if they were real friends, or if they just liked me for my peanut butter. They got it free, and they could even, if they wanted, swim in it, because of the big vats that were taken wholesale to the cafeterias and the sick wards, where people needed peanut butter to get better. Sometimes, they just waved as I drove by, and sometimes they turned away, because not remembering something good can hurt less than remembering it.

❊

Jettisoned against the sky, his ankles were weighted in water. So he was in between sky and water all the time, and he didn't like it, and he had breasts, which was strange to him, because he didn't think he should. But his friends said, "It's okay, man, some of us have breasts," and so he tried not to question whether or not he should. Anyway, he liked his friends, and he thought it was nice of them to feel him through this the way they did, understanding what he'd need when he realized that he had breasts and they did not. His friend Hank said, "Well some guys got man boobs," and Villandros, our protagonist, said, "No. These are real and actual breasts. Like I have touched on other people." And Hank said, "You mean on women," and Villandros said, "Is that what they're called?" Sometimes people jeered at him, people who read his story and didn't believe that he might not know the difference between the sexes, that there were two, and that he was a man. Mostly. People could be so cruel. But he kept at it, this imagining of himself as normal, as someone who was not a freak for being jettisoned, and not a freak for having parts that seemed like they ought to belong to someone else, or that were garish, somehow, on him. So he was grateful for their kindness, and not angry, and sometimes he looked into the water and saw how beautiful it was, and how beautiful his body looked beneath it, and he imagined that someday maybe he'd step outside the water, too, and see his body in the plain old air, and understand that it was good.

✳

Big shapes on the wall in screaming faces, pink, and some boobies, he says, and some fingers up assholes, he says, which he thought was great when he saw it in nineteen-ninety-nine. He laughs. Everyone else laughs. People laugh when they see fingers jammed up assholes. Dreams of childhood are red and pink and green and blue, and cartoonlike, and layered, everything layered—the shapes and the stand alones on the floor in front of the shapes, repeating themselves, maybe because memories repeat themselves, over and over in our lives, or maybe just because it is representing something that happened, which I do not know. This is art on the slide show, on the wall, this is art in the dark auditorium that was once a church. This is art in the green hills, in the dreamscape of a future I have wanted always, where nothing is hidden or too quiet, or fearful or ashamed.

WITH OBJECTS

There was a man with webbed toes, and a girl with starlet eyes, amber stars in the center of the brown, which glistened in the night. There was a troubadour-movie-maker who wore a red cape, and an armadillo who could speak, long pink tongue slipping forward on his s's. There was a killer whale with no top fin who was always flopping side to side in the water because he could not keep his balance. There was a kangaroo with no pouch, a dog missing half his tongue, a magician with no tricks up his sleeve, just an empty billowed piece of cotton dangling over his wrist, cuff open. In this place, no one had anything they wanted, or they lacked what they needed most, or they were simply strange. When visitors came by, they'd say it was all about perception, and how you saw yourself and on and on like this, but the ones who lived there felt the hole and knew it was a hole, and that no talking around it could make it feel less empty. Who would want a talking armadillo?

*

Soaked through, Avery came in from the rain. We told him, when
we saw him coming, that we didn't want him here. We even said
it in really loud voices: Avery! We DON'T WANT YOU HERE!
We screamed it from the deck, up on the hill, and we leaned over
the deck, and we said it until our voices were hoarse and our heads
were all wet from sticking them out in the rain and our stomachs
hurt from the top rail pressing into us. But maybe he couldn't hear
us. Or maybe he could and he was just so sad that he ignored us,
and kept on coming. We knew he had nowhere else to go. He was
Avery, skinny and slouched and always alone. Poor Avery. With his
hood over his head. He always wore his brother's shoes, hand-me-

downs, two sizes too big, and by the time he grew into them, he'd worn through the soles. So he had to switch up to the next pair. His brother was luckier than him; his brother grew so fast that he got new shoes every few months, and his shoes never wore out, and they always fit right. But if Avery wasn't ready for a pair yet, they were passed onto his cousins, and so Avery always got his brother's just-too-small shoes, and the not the several-pairs-ago pair that might have fit.

No one really knew why Avery was sad, why he slouched, why he was skinny, why he had black pools around his eyes underneath his skin, like that's where he was storing all the sadness. No one knew because he didn't talk, and that's why we didn't like him. We didn't like people who slouched and wouldn't explain why. We wanted to know the reason. We wanted to know what was his story, please. When we yelled at Avery, he didn't respond, and that made us more adamant. He should've known by now. He really should've.

When he came up onto the deck, his shoes went *klomp, klomp, klomp,* and they made a squishing sound as his foot lifted up. *Klomp-shhhhh! Klomp-shhhh!* Like his foot was pulling up all the water in the soles.

He walked onto the porch and Agatha said, What the heck, Avery? We said no Averies here.

And Avery looked down at her, and pinched his eyebrows together, and frowned in a way that looked like it was supposed to be a smile. He pulled his hood from his head and let the water drip off the hood and down his back. It splattered onto the backs of his calves, onto the blue deck. Our uncles painted this deck blue three years ago, and then they went out to sea to catch some lobsters and died. Now, our mother won't repaint the deck because she doesn't want to cover up any memories of her brothers, she says.

Yeah, said Thomas, get off, Avery, and Thomas walked forward and tried to look menacing. I saw him practicing this look in the mirror the other day, and making a little growling sound.

Avery leaned back, towards the long set of stairs that led back down to the street, where it was still raining. The rain made a sound like a river all around us.

Maybe he can stay, I said. Maybe it doesn't matter too much.

I didn't want Avery to fall down the stairs; I didn't want him to cry. His face was balling up into more and more of a grimace, or a look of consternation, as if he was on the verge and soon he would erupt. And when he erupted, he would melt, right here on our deck, into pools of black sadness like the pools underneath his eyes—it would all slip out from his body, at last, and we would see what a sack of sorrow he was, and wonder how he had held it all together for so long, anyway, with just the skin to cover the sorrow. So much of it. Just underneath. How he had even managed to move his legs and his arms and keep his neck up straight. That's what I saw, then, finally, after so much time of hollering at him—and maybe I had always seen it but I was afraid, and yelling was easier. It was what Thomas did. Agatha and I, we always did what Thomas did.

Avery cleared his throat. It made a sound like a robin chirping. We thought, here it comes, he'll speak. We waited. Later, we'd talk about how long we waited for him to talk, as if the rain stretched the moment into days and days. How our parents never guessed, when we went inside, that a lifetime had passed out on the deck. There they were, reading the paper and watching TV, my father's ankles crossed and my mother's tucked underneath her, and they didn't even realize the whole world had gone by. Avery opened his mouth. Avery closed his mouth. We all just watched.

Finally, after a long time of just listening to the rain and watching Avery very closely, Thomas said, WHAT? WHAT? You're making us CRAZY, AVERY!! And that made Agatha move closer, too, almost close enough to touch Avery. But she wasn't yelling anymore. She had her finger in her mouth. She is the youngest of us all, the most curious, the most likely to laugh. Avery kept opening and closing his mouth, and Thomas said, Goldfish! Goldfish! and puckered up his lips and copied Avery, turned his arms into fins, bent at the elbow with his hands underneath his armpits, and flapped them back and forth. Wiggled his butt as if it was a tail. Raised and lowered his head like he was diving. And Avery couldn't stop opening and closing his mouth. He was stuck, I could see, stuck in this motion, and the more Thomas mocked him, the more Avery was stuck, the more upset he looked, his eyebrows just one brow now, tears sliding down his cheeks, his mouth opening and closing and opening and closing, until it hurt me to watch, until it felt as if someone was yanking my own jaw opened and closed and opened and closed, and pressing very hard on the part of me that hurt the most—the being-afraid-of-the-dark part, the time-I-got-lost-at-the-fair-and-no one-noticed-for-hours part—I felt as if it was all slipping from somewhere inside me, up to my jaw, and back again, a big loop, a big loop of stuck.

Stop that, I said.

First it was very quiet, and no one heard. And Thomas kept doing it, and Avery kept doing what he was doing, and I said it again, very loud: STOP THAT! STOP IT STOP IT STOP IT! and I threw my hands in the air and stomped my feet and let myself wail. I let out everything, all at once. I spit out the carousel that I'd watched for an hour and the sheep that I'd sat beside while I watched all the strangers who weren't my parents walk past, and I'd wondered if I'd ever have a family again, and I spit out the nights I woke up most afraid and screamed for my mother to help me but she didn't come, maybe because I was screaming silent—those times you're so afraid your voice doesn't come out—or because she didn't hear or she didn't want to get out of bed, I don't know; I only know she didn't come, and I was so afraid, too afraid to get out of bed and walk down the hall and find her, so I could only cry myself to sleep.

Thomas laughed, and looked at Avery and said, Yeah! And I got quiet, then, and I looked straight at Thomas, and I said, No, you. YOU, Thomas, you stop. And I pointed at him, and I even leaned forward and let my finger almost touch his shoulder, like I might push if he provoked me, like I wasn't scared at all. He was wearing his pink flamingo shirt. And he turned to me and looked at me with his own jaw open, like he couldn't believe what I had done, and the rain kept falling, and Agatha watched us with her finger in her mouth, her black hair all frizzy around her face like it always is in the rain.

I stared at Thomas. He put his arms down. He closed his mouth. He looked back at me, and when he did, I saw he was ashamed. It was the first time I ever saw him look that way. Agatha turned to Avery. I tried to catch my breath, my chest going up and down, my heart beating fastfastfast, because I was so afraid just then, doing what I'd never had the courage to do before. And it had worked. And I was stunned.

I saw, out of the corner of my eye, Agatha, who reached out to touch Avery. She pressed her hand to his jaw, and let it stay there. It was a reach for her, to get to his jaw. I turned to watch. He closed his mouth. He kept his eyes on us, but he could feel her, we knew. We all just breathed. And then this miracle happened, and his lips turned up.

*

Finally, there was an avalanche in his heart, and his heart opened to it, instead of closing, which is what most hearts would do. The avalanche was gray and thick and full of rocks and angles, and it hurt his heart, but he refused to close the valves or reroute the avalanche to his arm or leg, where maybe it would hurt less. Someone had promised him that if he left his heart open, the avalanche would melt into something softer, and flow easy into his bloodstream, and loosen into nothing. He didn't know if he believed this person. It didn't make much sense, and it was all so much hurting, all this hurting, on and on and on, hurting endlessly. But, what could he do? The avalanches kept coming and he was tired of diverting them to his legs and arms. His legs and arms were all bruised and battered on the inside, and sore. Everything was sore. He couldn't walk up hills anymore. He couldn't hold his child. He couldn't sing songs in the open air, with his arms spread wide. He said, "I am left with nothing, so what do I have to lose by opening my heart? Nothing." Then he played some Janis Joplin and sang about freedom, and laughed at himself a little. So he let the avalanche come, and he waited for the ricocheting rock and the way the capillaries and arteries and veins felt like they were coming apart, and the way the various compartments of his heart felt like they were tearing and cutting and slicing open, so that maybe his whole heart would fall apart and he would be a body without a heart and he would die, because a body without a heart is nothing. But he said, "This is just the avalanche. It isn't *really* breaking apart my body." And he withstood it. And he waited. And then, after a very long time—most of his life and his child's life and his wife's life combined—the avalanche began to lose its corners and its sharpness and its cut, and it began to melt, and since he had endured these avalanches for a lifetime, and since he had spent a lifetime diverting them and rerouting them and looking for ways to manage and avoid them, and since at last, he had opened his heart to them and felt all the pain he'd avoided all those years—three thousand years of pain—when the avalanche abated, and his heart was still beating (ka-thump, ka-thump, ka-thump) as every living heart does, and he was still alive and his family was still alive and no older than when he'd started to let the avalanche run through his heart, he never, ever ever ever ever *ever* felt so good.

*

They gave us eyeglasses instead of ears, and we thought, This is all wrong. We ordered ears and we got these lenses and sticks? When we called them to tell them about the error, they said, You'll have to speak to our cleaning department, and we didn't understand that, either. We said the world is unjust and life is unfair and we're really pissed off at you now. They said, Tell that to our neurologist; she's always saying how unfair life is. We asked why they had a company neurologist, and they couldn't answer. We asked where we were calling, and they said, Where are you calling from, and we said, Johnson, Vermont, and they said, That explains everything. And then they hung up.

✻

Someone said this would work, the avalanching—trust, he said, believe me. So Albert had. He had opened up his heart to the avalanches. He had believed that it would work. What did he have to lose? Nothing, his life had become nothing; he was desperate for a cure. And it had worked, that was true. But all along, the someone who had told him this, that someone was holding apple pies beneath his desk, and devouring them, and delighting in their flavor—all while Albert talked about the avalanches, and how they hurt, and how he longed for something sweet like pie, for something good. And when Albert caught a glimpse of apple crumb on the someone's cheek, he looked away, because he thought: no, no, that would be too strange, for someone to be eating pie while I am talking of the pie I'd love. But then, it kept happening, and when he stared too long at the crumb, the someone would turn away and blush and act funny—scratching his arms, always, or rubbing his fingers in his hair. And finally, Albert said, "It's pie, isn't it? You have pie." And the someone looked down and said, "Yes," and Albert said, "Why have I done all of this? Why have I confessed all of this to you, a pie eater?" And he felt as though the avalanches came and came and came, and finally, his heart did break, after all, because there were too many rocks at once. There was too much pain. There is a way of overdoing it, and now, with the pie, it was done. There lay Albert, there on the floor, looking as if he'd been stoned from the inside out, an escaped boulder lying on the pea-green rug beside his chin.

take
WAY??
(I wish you could
take it away.)

*

I am a shed, holding old rakes and rusting shovels. I am a shed that no one needs now. The people who needed me, once, have moved away. I live in Maine, and I am made for helping with the snow, and the lawn, and the children's outdoor toys. The children used to laugh around me, and play behind me, and climb onto my roof (when they were older) and smoke joints and drink beer. And I liked the company. But now I am just a shed with no people, and I hold things that are just objects because they are not in use. When they were in use, they were tools. Soon, they will disintegrate into pieces of themselves — metal, rusted out, wood, rotted. Someday, I will disintegrate into nothing. The spring will come, and I will feel the snow melt from me, and with it will go little pieces of my siding, first splinters and then larger bits, and then my roof, and then my frame, and the termites and the carpenter ants will find me, and I will be all toothless and solitary, dripping apart in the springtime, and I will keep hoping to be found, that someone will buy the house and take me up again, and put me back together. I will hope for a short spring, for a long, dry summer. I will hope for clear skies. I will hope for the sound of footsteps, which I will feel echoing through the ground, coming towards me. Thud, thud, thud. Their thunder meaning hope.

*

When they were small, they didn't understand the way words went with things—with objects, with feelings, with sounds, with colors. And it was so hard to remember, how words went, and what was just said, and what it signified. No one could keep it straight in this land, and so they all sank deeper and deeper into wordlessness, and there were only blurry movements, a heartbeat over and over, the clanking of a stick onto a top or into air, into nothing, and there were squalls and shrieks and cries and all these sounds of anguish, filling up the air. And the people kept on sinking and sinking, because they didn't know any way out of it, out of the wordlessness, and when the others came to visit and shaped their lips this way and made the sounds that way, the people who were wordless just got angry. There was no way to bridge the gap. There was no way to get what they wanted, which was the object or the hug or the snack. Maybe what they wanted most of all was to understand each other, to know which word came next, to be able to say: this is how I feel, and to not feel so much pain just pushing out those words. So instead of speaking, they gave their pain shapes and symbols: a thousand strands of string tied to everything in the house, at waist level, in the middle of the night. So when the others woke up, they would see the repetition, and know that it meant pain. Or sorrow. Or desire. Or sadness. Or hope. The people who were wordless would not do what they were told, because they could not associate the commands with the action, so they cried instead, they beat their hands into clapping sounds instead, they banged their heads into the wall instead. And the others understood that this was anguish, how much it hurt, how much the people wished there was another way, now that they had seen that there was. Until the others came, the people who were wordless were okay with sinking, with darkness, with motion and abstraction and the blurring of things—a streak of a red shirt dashing through the air—and they didn't need words. They didn't need anything other than what they had, and they thought that all of the aloneness that they felt was just the way that things were meant to be. The others, though, would sit in things that moved back and forth, and put things to their lips, and laugh. They would make sounds that didn't sound like crying, and they would move their bodies in ways that didn't look like jerks or frights or pinwheels. So the people who were wordless began to watch the others, to imitate the way they sat on chairs—to learn that they were called chairs—to rock back and forth when the sun went down, to drink lemonade, to drink beer, to eat the things that were good that were called pasta and egg rolls and tabouli, to talk to one another and listen to the words that were sent back in talking, and to understand that they all felt the same things, and that there were ways of speaking to each other and understanding that they all felt the same things, and that there were words like empathy and sympathize and discussion and disagree and concur. There were words like requiem and vitriol and solipsistic and diagram and heart. And they began to laugh, and to feel the laughter, and to be able to say, "I feel happy," because they did. And then there was no difference, anymore, between the others and the people who used to be wordless. They were the same. There was no spectrum. No identification. No signifying difference. And one of the people said, "I wish there was a way for everyone to feel this good, to never go through that pain, to never have to recover language." And all the people nodded, and sipped their lemonade, and leaned into each other.

*

We made the deer of paper, covered in words, because we wanted them to know what they were. So, we wrapped them in stories, and they could read to each other at night, and understand that they were "deer," because there was the word "deer" right there on their rump, or their neck, or their hoof. And there was snow all around them, so they were camouflaged, with the white paper and the white snow, and they were safe that way.

We always wanted them to be safe, that's why we made them. That's why we set them in such a pretty place, so they could cherish it and it could cherish them. They were surrounded by crests and hills and acres of snow, and they could wander through it whenever they liked.

They said, though, that the one thing they really missed was having snouts and nostrils.

"We're very grateful for our bodies," they said, "but we wish we could smell the world, you know? We are tired of reading and not being able to smell, and taste, and understand it. We don't understand it if we can't take it in in every way. Do you know?"

And we said, "We understand. We can smell, yeah, we know just what you mean. Pine trees aren't pine trees without the odor."

"But," said the best-read deer, "A rose by any other name — Doesn't that work with smells, too? Is it the naming that makes the thing or the smell or the shape? What makes the thing the thing it is?"

And we said, "Now you have really stumped us. We weren't ready for a discussion of philosophy. We underestimated you. We watched Bambi one too many times. It isn't all ice skating, is it? You really sank your teeth into this, this cognition thing."

And the deer cocked their heads and smirked a little, and looked offended.

"Uh, yeah," said the teenaged deer, and then he muttered, under his breath, "Dumbasses," and we heard, and ignored it, because

we had done them a disservice and neglected to give them a part—
nostrils, to smell. Which meant we'd short-changed them two senses:
taste and smell. Which meant they could not have the whole world.
And they were not really safe. They needed to smell for their food,
beneath the snow. They needed to smell for the coyotes in the night,
to run before they were caught.

So, we reconvened, in the big conference room with the bad lighting (we hate fluorescent lights but are sticking with them for now, to save on energy costs), and we sat around the big oval table that has no seams, and we talked about how to fashion snouts.

Edgar said, "Just poke holes into the paper," and Jenine said, "It's too late for that; their bodies have developed beyond just the paper. They are their own selves now. We have to mold something, from clay, and find a way to fasten it."

"Glue," said Bennie, and we looked at Bennie and wondered for the thousandth time how he got such long fingers and such a short body. We never asked, though, because it seemed rude.

Finally, Nadine spoke up and said, "I say we let them make their own noses. Let's let them decide what they want, and how they want it done. Right?"

And we looked at each other and nodded, and said, "Sure, if they're thinking theory, they can think design."

We got up from the table and turned off the lights and left the room. Dark. We all walked home, and wondered what we'd make for dinner. Our stomachs were growling.

The next day, we approached the deer and asked them what they thought, and they nodded their dainty deer heads and spun their ears toward us and then to each other, and then the littlest one, the teenaged one said, "Yeah, we already figured it out. Last night."

We said, "Oh, wonderful! And?"

They said, "We're going to take your noses, and graft them to our bodies. It's the only way to get the nerves and skin and everything we need to connect the nose to the brain, to make it work. What do you say?"

Our stomachs fell from our torsos to our feet, and we sat and looked at them, and realized we'd been outsmarted by the deer. And that we could not say no because we'd made them without noses, and made them suffer without noses for years, and hadn't even considered this dilemma before, until they brought it up.

"Shit," said Nadine. "Shit shit shit."

Edgar said, "*Hell*, no."

Bennie pushed his long fingers together and said, "They're right."

We knew they were, even though we did not want to admit it.

"How much longer can we keep our noses?" we said.

The deer said, "Three days."

We said, "Okay."

And now, even though we'd made them, the deer were in charge. This is always the way. Ask any robot.

We decided to make the most of our last three days with scent and taste, and we went on eating binges, and drank thousand-dollar bottles of wine, and stuffed our noses into lilies and into our spouses' hair and into their bodies. We smelled the rain and the sun and the dirt and the pizza and the steak. We smelled the eggs and the fresh apples and the baked apples and the smoke from the fires we made at night. We smelled everything, and we smelled everything so hard that, although we did not know it, the smells traveled up into our brains in little tiny particles, and rested there, in little compartments labeled "lilies," and "pizza," and "Jackie, my wife's body," and "Larry's running socks." We began to realize that we would miss even the bad smells, and we smelled those, too. Rotten eggs, old coffee rinds, house paint. Everything. The trash, the grass, each other's feet.

Three days later, there we were, before the deer. They put on their surgical masks and scrubbed into the surgery room.

We said, "Hold on, how will you cut with those hooves?"

The oldest one looked at us and said, "Don't worry, you won't feel a thing, you'll be out."

Then, they put the masks over our faces, and we were out. And when we woke up, we still had our faces and our noses and looked exactly the same, and we wondered if they'd taken pity on us, if they'd left us our sense of smell. We looked out the window from our beds, though, and saw them dancing outside, and putting their noses to the branches and the berries and the coyote poop and the nuts, and we knew that they had taken our smell, and we would be without it for the rest of our lives. We touched our bandaged noses and wondered when we'd realize that we were without it. One of the deer came in, a white apron wrapped around her body, and she gave us packs of ice to put on our faces, even though our faces didn't hurt at all and we still felt unchanged.

She said, "For the psychic pain," and we took the ice packs.

Nadine said, "How long until we can take the bandages off, until we know we don't have smell?"

The deer said, "One day."

She looked sorry for us, and looked out at the deer gallivanting in the snow, and walked out again, hooves clacking on the tile floor. We saw her a few minutes later, outside, telling them all to go away. They looked in at us, and remembered what had happened, and walked off into the snow, very quiet.

The next day, we took the bandages off, and we walked out of the hospital. We all breathed through our mouths because we were so afraid of the heartbreak that we knew would come when we realized that our smell was gone, when we really felt it. We knew how much emptier our lives would be without it, and without taste, and we tried to tell ourselves, "Well, this is how it's supposed to be, then. This is our new life." But it didn't work. We were all slouched and sad. We were all so sad.

Finally, Edgar closed his mouth, out in the parking lot, and took one big breath in through his nose.

He turned to us. We waited for a shout, a cry, some sorrow, a tantrum. His eyes were wide, wide open.

"Do it," he said. "Breathe in."

So we all closed our mouths, and took big breaths in through our noses, and waited. And looked at each other, wondering, Could it be? And we tried it one more time. And we thought: Are we imagining? Is it just wishful thinking, that we are smelling? But, no, we were smelling! There was the smell of snow, and the smell of pine, and the smell of each other, sweating and afraid, and then delighted. We realized that everything smelled, and that there was no way to separate the thing from its smell or its color or its shape, that it needed everything to be itself, and that we needed every sense to know the world, to know ourselves, to know each other. We hugged each other and smelled each other's happiness, which rose from our bodies like steam, like we'd just been running in the cold and our bodies were giving off heat. That's how the smell would look.

We thought, We are not bereft of smell or taste! We are all right! We are still whole!

We laughed and hugged and danced around the parking lot, whooping, for so long that the deer emerged from the woods and stood at the perimeter of the lot, the farthest they could go, and watched us, wondering. Inquisitive. With their new noses, their new whole bodies, the completion of joy.

That night, exhausted from eating and smelling, we realized what must have happened, the way we stored up all the memories in our brains, the way the particles lasted, and the way the particles could combine and shift depending on what we smelled, if it was something new that was not compartmentalized already in our brains. So we had smell, all smells, and taste, all tastes. And we were not bereft or robbed of something that we needed. We realized that senses are not luxuries. And that memories are the same as senses, that we might have been tricking ourselves after all, but that it did not matter because it felt real. We had smell. We could taste. And we were delighted with ourselves and delighted with the deer and delighted with the world. And for the next week, we had a fire in the woods, with the deer, our first party with the herd, and wondered why we'd never mingled before, and we talked about Derrida and Chaucer and Woolf and Stein and Picasso, and were astounded at what they knew.

Timeless Treasures Fabrics,Inc. © All Rights Reserved. patt# FLEUR-C 4794

❃

She was always cutting these pieces off of me, and this was at a time
when I did not know that I could tell her: "Don't cut that piece off."
So I let too much of myself go. First, before she cut, she burned.
She'd focus on each little circle, raised bumps on my body, all over
my body — behind my knees and at my hips and all along my stom-
ach. Sometimes they ran in rows. Sometimes they were sporadic.
Sometimes I saw pictures in their shapes, and the pictures would
emerge the way constellations do when you look with someone who
knows more than you do about the sky, and he points out each star,
and then says, "See? A pogo stick," and you say, "Ahhhh." It was
like that, except that it was my own body I was looking at, and I
didn't like the dots. They were ugly and shameful, and I knew I was
the only one who had them and I did not understand why I had to
get them. I thought that I must be very bad to get to the dots. Finally, after months of being burned and cut, I was so tired, and I had
all these dark circular scars across my skin, and my skin was sore,
and always bleeding a little, covered in band aids and tinged yellow from the disinfectant, and I was always worried about when the
new dots would appear. I would check the mirror each morning to
see: Had I gotten any more? Oh, crud, yes, three. I would call her
and she would say, "Come on in and we'll burn and slice you," and
I wouldn't tell any of my friends because I was so ashamed of my
dots. I slid off to see her in secret, and had my dots cut in secret, and
then covered the wounds with bandages and pants and long-sleeved
shirts. And finally, I thought, There must be some other solution
here. This is archaic. And it was archaic. It was nineteen-eighty-
eight, for crying out loud. I was close to being bled. Leeches. Those
old stories you hear. So I found a man who specialized in little dots
across the body, especially the raised dots — he'd done a study of
it, over the course of twenty years, and published the study in the
extremely prestigious journal published by the Academy of Dots and
Dermatological Malformations. I found it in the library, and it was

a surprise because I did not know that there was a study about this, or a school that taught people about it, or even a library that held all these secrets that could unlock me, that could save me. I always thought the library was the same as the fire station. Brick. With sirens inside. And once I knew that there were other people out there with dots, I began to feel less ashamed, and less all alone in my bandages and long-sleeved shirts even through the summertime. I called the man who published the study, and I said, "I think I have the dots you wrote about," and he said, "Tell me a little bit about yourself," and I said, "Well, I am ten, and I go to Drew Elementary." He said, "All right, I'll see you." We made an appointment. And when I saw him, in my little white gown that was opened in the back, he looked at my dots, and touched them with his fingers—not even with gloves on like the other woman had, when she burned me and looked disgusted by my dots—and he said, "Yup, these are dots all right." And I said, "How will you take them off of me?" And he looked at me for a long time, and I saw that he was a very old and very kind man, because he did not look away, not once, even though he knew that I could be carrying this disease around with me through the world, could be passing it on to all the other people in the world. He said, "Look down." And I did, and I saw: all my constellations had bloomed into flowers, dogwood white scattered on my body, around my belly button, up each leg, winding across my hips and up to my back. And I cried because it was beautiful and not those ugly dots I'd always known. And then, as I kept looking, the flowers started to fade, and disappear into the air, and I cried, and all that was a left was skin. So I was just myself, a regular ten year old again, maybe for the first time in my life. "How did you do that?" I said. And he said, "You were misinformed. It was buds, waiting to bloom." And I said, "So they didn't have to cut them off of me, all this time? And burn me? And try to kill little slices of me, shave them off bit by bit?" The old man shook his head and looked sad, and touched his forehead with one hand. He said, "If only all the people knew. Are you scared now?" I said, "No, not anymore. I wouldn't even mind if they came back." He nodded. "That's the point," he said. "That's why they're gone." And then I was in my clothes, and on the street with the big elm trees overhead, and I was walking home, feeling strange and naked and light.

*

59

The nests are made of rope, and sit in clusters on the floor, and they are small enough for just a single bird, a small one: a chickadee. Hanging from the ceiling are pieces of metal, gouged? Shaped? They are delicate, like leaves. She says, It is about presence and absence. She says, This one is more literal than the first. The second picture is of a wax rectangle, with circles taken out of it, and on the floor are the circles, shaped into bowls. She says, People save things in bowls. There are big sheets of metal that have been melted or mixed with other metal so that their surfaces are all bubbled and burned. There are shapes on the floor that look like leaves, dusted in rust, dusted in sand, and wax mixed with sand, and it makes me want to walk into the shapes, and settle in their midst on the floor, and be very quiet.

SAVOR, SALVE, RED SLIVERS

*

63

On the floor, I find first my heart — beige with gold lines through it —
and then, that tiny-flowered brown print — my head. The other day,
a bright green blade of grass, and stuck to my dog's chin, the hand I
could not find when I was putting together my body. Sometimes, I'll
find remnants of a woman's yellow-flowered hair, a discarded gold-
print leg that was the wrong shape, a too-oblong foot. Scattered all
around — in the living room, or stuck to my sock, found just before
bedtime.

❋

Once, there was a man named Herman, and he was tall and thin.
Herman wanted a wife. He had had a wife, but she had died. And
now he wanted another wife — or, he wanted his old wife back,
but knew this was impossible, and was willing to *settle for* a new
wife.

His daughter was named Bee, and she didn't approve — not of
her father wanting a new wife, and not of his being willing to settle
for someone other than her mother. It was a disservice, she said, to
this new woman. She would argue with her father, with Herman,
and Herman would shut his ears.

Herman had ear valves, and he could slide them open and
closed when he licked his lips, and he was the envy of all his long-
married friends.

Bee had no talents, and she was angry about this. Her mother,
Ebony, had been able to walk just above the ground, on the air,
not enough so that people would notice but just enough so that she
never felt the hardness of the ground. She was always protected that
way, cushioned by air as she walked, and Herman said this is what
made her so gentle. Anyone who had never felt the hardness of this
world was bound to be a little kinder than the rest of us. He said.
Bee thought it was just Ebony's nature to be kind, and Bee wished
she had gotten that, too. Instead, Bee was cantankerous. A big jowl
face. Her father would cluck and shake his head and tell her the
jowls would shrink if only she would lighten herself a little, if only
she would smile.

Which came first? Bee would say, and her father would slide
his ear valves shut. Bee heard them seal with a little *shoosh* sound.

Sometimes, Bee walked in the garden in the city, a rose garden,
because this was a lush city with a good deal of rain and not much
snow, and the roses flourished here. The name of the city was Port-

land, and just beyond, there were great tall trees that grew in a forest full of water and rain, and Bee and Ebony, when Bee was small and Ebony was alive, would bring peanut-butter and honey sandwiches to the forest, and run to a mossy place, and sit down to eat, and dare each other to try to get their arms around a whole tall tree. That reached up to the sky, to the clouds, to places where the world was only what it was and not so full of all these meanings and relationships. Bee did not like relationships, not even when she was small.

Bee's best friend was a boy named Fuster, which Bee's father said was not a good sign. Bee met Fuster when she was in first grade, and she had a lisp and called him Futh-ter. Finally, she began to call him Grim, because there were no s's, and he was a very dark boy. This is why she liked him.

Bee and Grim went to the shore together every year with Grim's family. They took Bee along because she seemed to cheer Grim up, even though she called him this name—they thought, Well, she is a little girl and she likes make believe and she is his friend, and he has no other friends, so if she teases him just a little, well, all right. She did not tease him unkindly. She made him laugh at himself, and he did her, too. He called her Mutton face, because he'd heard his father call her that once (when Bee was not around), and he thought that was mean, but when he told Bee that he had argued about it with his father, Bee had just laughed and said, *Baaaaa*.

Then Grim laughed, too, and Bee told him why he was laughing—because mutton is old lamb. Call me that, she said. I want that to be my nickname. Okay, said Grim.

Grim didn't tell her that when she laughed, his insides flew into sparks.

Grim and Bee grew up together, and went to the sea each year, and spent a week playing cards by gas lamps and waking up early to play hide and seek at low tide, crouching behind the big boulders at the water's edge. Which black rock is Bee behind? She would squat, breathless, behind the farthest one, having run through ankle-deep water so she'd leave no prints, her pant legs pressed up against her bottom, her chest heaving, her cheeks all flushed. She'd press her hands to her face and hold her cheeks, hold her jaw, and lean her head back and look up at the sky, where the clouds moved out to sea, or back to land from wherever they'd been on the edge of the world, the other side of the world, from China, raining down far-away stories on all of Oregon.

And Grim would creep up very quietly, and breathe against her neck until she turned her head to see him, and he would crouch beside her, and they would breathe in the wet sand, side by side, wishing for the sort of gifts her parents had, and knowing that they were just two ordinary strange children in this great big world of clouds and rocks and trees and sea—and all of it, always, moving.

Herman would call Bee on Saturdays, now, from his home in California. He had moved away because he could not stand to live in the place in which he always lived with his wife, the love of his life. All those memories, he'd say, they are too much. They are everywhere. Well, said Bee, then why try to stopgap them with a new wife? Why not just let the memories be and go on with what you have?

Herman had never understood his daughter. It wasn't the funny way she had of talking—he understood the *words*—it was that her logic was not the same as his, and that made for another language, as if she'd filled her life with some other forms of life.

Values, Grim would say, are not compromisable.

Bee still called Grim for comfort, and he would give her these sorts of vague phrases, and she did not understand where he got them. Sometimes she wanted to shout, Where is the *old* Grim? Where is the Grim who says things like, *Cheese is the enemy of the state* and breathed with me and watched the sky?

And her father would say into the phone, Why don't you marry that Grim, anyway? Aren't you two in love? I want you to find love, Bee, and your mother did, too.

And Bee would say, Thank you for your kind thoughts. I am closing my *proverbial* ear valves now.

And she would hope her father heard the emphasis, and remember that he had not given her any of the family's magic, and hang up the phone.

Grim lived on the other side of Portland, so on rainy days, they would walk to meet each other in the middle, in the rose garden, which is what they loved most in the world. They never went to the coast anymore because Grim's parents had died there, one fall, when Grim was away at aviator weekend camp. The old electricity-less house was still there, seemingly hovering at the edge of the cliff (but firmly rooted in rock, with steel cords and screws).

So they had the rose garden, and they would sit on a bench and push at the grass and the puddles with the tips of their rain boots, and brush shoulders, and talk.

Why do you think the stars are falling? Bee would say.

And Grim would say, Your father just wants to feel happy again, like he was with your mother.

And Bee would say, There is a hole in the center of the sea, and all the water spins into the hole, and then all the water is pushed back out again, and that's what makes the waves.

No, Grim would say, the waves are made because the earth's plates are moving. You know this. You know this, Bee. Stop pretending.

Bee didn't know what Grim meant when he said that.

Yes, you *do*, he would say. You do know.

I didn't say anything, said Bee.

You did, said Grim. I heard.

Sometimes Bee was tired of everything—of hearing and not hearing of seeing and not seeing of loving and not loving. Sometimes all of it was a burden, and she wanted to close herself off from the world.

Not to leave it, only to close herself off for a little while and stop *feeling* it. Sometimes the feeling was such a thing to carry! She did not see why Grim didn't see this, why he wouldn't want to go to the old house on the cliff without any manmade lights or sounds, but just the sea and the sky and the big tall trees, and stay there for awhile, just the two of them, until they both felt better.

Her father said, This is what love is—wanting to go to a house just the two of you.

Bee would say, It isn't love to want silence.

You don't want silence, he'd tell her. That isn't what you want. That's not the gift you got.

No, she'd say, I got mutton.

You got love, he'd say. You got love, Bee. You just can't use it because you're so afraid, and wishing for some other thing.

And she would turn scarlet and say, That's a ridiculous thing to say, and she'd roll her eyes, like a child, and hang up the phone or walk away, whichever was appropriate, depending on her location (visiting her father in California or talking to him by phone from Portland).

Grim had once fallen in love with a girl named Bev, and Bee had hated Bev. Bev was very tall with long blond hair and big button-blue eyes, shiny and plastic, and a hee-haw laugh. When Grim fell in love with Bev, he was seventeen, and Bee's mother Ebony was still alive.

Ebony took Bee to the forest, where they hadn't been for a very long time, and they sat and had peanut-butter and honey sandwiches, and Ebony said, Can you get your arms around that one? And Bee lay back against the moss and said, Mmm, and didn't try.

Bee stared up at the treetops, which did not sway today because there was no wind. The trees drove straight up to the sky, big fat trunks, they did not bend or sway, they just grew as if they always knew where they were going: up. And they kept on going. That was the thing about a tree, how it would never stop. A reaching thing, a sort of certainty and faith and always wanting.

Do you like Bev? said her mother.

Bee scrunched up her nose. Eh, she said. She has those creepy eyes.

He waited for *you*, said Ebony, but you're afraid.

Bee looked at her mother, whose cheeks were red with the hike.

Mom, she said. It was a word she hardly ever used. She hadn't any need for it, because her mother was always there and always listening and always waiting for Bee to come to her and tell her some news of her life. Her mother was the sort of mother that other girls, who did not have mothers, or who had disinterested or hard mothers, wished they had.

One day, said Ebony, you'll try.

I like the way the moss feels against my neck, said Bee. And she sighed and closed her eyes.

And two days later, her mother was dead. Sometimes Bee can still hear the sound of tires screeching. She tries to replace that sound, in her mind, with the sound of the wind, and the feel of the moss against her neck — soft. She is always pushing against something — memories, feelings, sounds — trying to erase these things and fill herself with what was good. What is still good.

Herman called Bee one day in June, when it was warm and all the flowers bloomed—a city full of pink and red blossoms.

Yes? said Bee.

It is tomorrow, said Herman.

No.

I mean for the wedding, it is tomorrow.

No.

Yes, Bee, yes. And you will bring Grim. You will come to California with Grim. I have sent Alistair for you.

Alistair was the cook, a man her father hired after Ebony died, because Herman had stopped eating and could not function any longer like that, dwindling to nothing. So now Alistair would help by driving Bee home (because she did not like to fly or drive herself). Grim would not drive, either. He'd never gotten his license. His parents had died a month after Bee's mother died, when he was away at aviator camp, with Bev, and he took that as a sign that he should not navigate moving objects. Or be with Bev.

And anyway, he didn't love Bev. It was just a way of being close to someone—to do the things they did—but it wasn't what he really wanted. Everyone knew that, even Grim. Maybe even Bee.

Her name, the new wife, was Vermillion, and Herman said he loved her very much. He said she was a wonderful woman— *wonderful*—and that Bee would grow to love her, too. Grow. Bee stored up these words and spit them out at Grim later, in the bedroom, complaining.

But at the wedding, she was cordial. It was in Napa, and it was beautiful—the hills and the vineyard in the background and the vases of daisies everywhere.

Where did your name come from, Vermillion? said Bee.

Grim nudged her. He'd heard the way she said it: Ver*mill*ion.

My grandmother, she said, who said that's how I looked when I came out of the womb! And then she laughed and tossed her head back, the way people do in movies, and held her wine glass in her dainty fingers. And Herman walked up behind her and put his hands around her waist and they swayed side to side and smiled. And Bee thought: Well, he is happy.

Still, though, she complained. She complained and complained and complained, and Grim listened.

He sat on the other bed, both double beds in the hotel room, which their father had booked for them—not two rooms, thought

Bee, but one—and Grim smiled at her, and said, Your head is in the way of your life, Bee.

My face, she said.

Not your face. Your head. Your face is beautiful.

My face is mutton, and I got nothing special from that magic line. No floating feet, no trick ears. Just some big jowls. A mutton face. Maybe I'm not even from the same family. Maybe they picked me up somewhere, took the wrong baby home—you know, those stories.

She knew that she was whining. She wished herself to stop, but this sadness had floated up in her, and she missed the old Grim, and she couldn't stop herself.

Oh, Bee.

Oh, Grim.

Don't mock.

I don't mock. I slight.

I love you.

Silence, then. Came silence. And all the trees in the world swayed while Bee thought, her breath caught in her throat, her heart caught in her chest, her head caught in her eyes—staring up at the ceiling, where she'd flopped onto the bed.

She breathed. She breathed. She thought of her mother, that day in the woods.

Nothing is that simple, she said. That's not a cure for anything.

Earlier, at the reception, they'd eaten cake from white china plates and danced on a wooden floor set onto grass, a hill that sloped to the vineyard, and the sun went down behind those vines. It was cold. She'd taken off her shoes just to feel the dew gathering on the wood, to make sure her skin was alive.

I'm ten thousand acres of sand, he said.

More quiet. The room was falling, Bee was sure. The hotel was tipping forward and sliding down the hill. It was midnight. These things happened at midnight.

He said, Now do you see?

I left footprints, she said. And her voice was soft but not quiet, not at all.

And then she smiled, and he knew that someday, it would be all right.

It's so hot in here, she said. God, I hate how hot it is. I'm going to open a window. I love you. I'm going to find the air.

It was more than he expected, tonight, and there was a rush inside of him. He sat on the bed, listening to her move. The stomp of her feet on the wood floor. He loved the sound of her moving. He loved the sound of what everyone thought was her anger, which was not anger at all but her way of finding the world. She liked to make sure it was always under her, that it would hold. She liked to stomp into it.

And she walked to the window, and she pushed the curtains back, and pushed the panes out, so that the air blew in, and she thought: This is the air from China, and it's blowing its stories onto us, and Grim thought the same thing, at the same time.

✻

He erases what he made twenty years ago, and then layers on other things. He is layering and unlayering to find what he knew then. He sands it down. He wipes it clean with paint thinner, the weaker kind, the more unpredictable kind, to see what it will do. He rubs the paper so hard that it tears, and sometimes he patches the tears and sometimes he doesn't. He hides the faces of the people he painted then, and he covers them with new faces. In one, with a red mouth, he says he is alluding to someone else, a painter who always uses red.

He draws ponds with concentric circles made by ducks. He draws a stump over and over again. Some paintings are seven feet long, some paintings are twenty-two inches by twenty-two inches. He draws bathtubs with women in them, sculpts a bathtub with asbestos fiber, because it's what they were given then, and then, thirty years later, he paints an empty bathtub. All the bathtubs are white and deep and old-fashioned, as if they might have claw feet. He used to love film, when he was in high school, was obsessed with film, B-movies, he loves this B-movie star and dedicated a seven-foot-long strip to her, with words written in black ink and pictures of her face. He'd sit in his room alone and act out the films, with make-up and everything.

Says he used to always be alone in his room, so he got used to being alone—then says, "That isn't true. I don't know why I just said that."

He says he erases things because he didn't know enough then about composition. "I liked the angle of her head, but I didn't know how to paint her face," and then, thirty years later, he paints her face.

He says, "Do you ever have the feeling, you know, 'everything went to shit in nineteen eighty-nine when I added that daub of purple paint. From then on, it was all ruined'?"

He laughs. He says that is why he goes back. He can remove

the purple paint. He can add something better. He says that's a painting of the woman he married. He doesn't call her his wife, until later. She doesn't like to be painted because she's always moving.

He's lived in the city and in the country, and his paintings change according to his place. There is that stump, over and over again. When the professor in the audience says the chairs and the bathtubs are about his solitude, his aloneness, he nods and says, "Mm, that's gratifying that you saw that. I don't see that. I only see my father." For a long time, he says, the chairs had to be empty, and now, he's able to put a man in the paintings, because he's come further along. And in the seventies, when he was having that hard time with his life and his work and where was he going with it all, he said, "And I was seeing a shrink, and the shrink said, " (he puts on a walkie-talkie voice, cartooned and crackly), "'Do you want to make art or don't you?'" And he laughs, and says, "So I was dealing with all this shit. And I was supposed to be drafted and I was very naïve and thought, you know, I'll go to prison. And I couldn't last in prison. So, I got out of it because —" a pause, he laughs, cocks his head to one side, "I convinced them I was crazy." He laughs harder. He says, "And then I decided, well, I think I'd want to paint even if none of this stuff was ever seen. So I painted again, and made a painting every night, because I couldn't deal with these big projects then."

He goes through one hundred slides in an hour and the room is dark, and the last painting is Porky the Pig. Some people don't like the way he engages with art history, he says. He says he makes little paintings as he's making the big paintings, and some of the paintings are "dead horses," and some are "fellow travelers" of the bigger paintings. So the empty chairs and empty bathtubs are never alone.

When he turns off the studio lights late at night, and goes home, and the canvases are sore from their erasure and the adding of paint, or of being restretched so he could expand the picture, all this change, over time, then they have each other, and talk in the darkness.

❊

There was a man who lived on a mattress in the Gold Dust Room, a place that could be rented for a small fee. He dragged his mattress out at night to sleep and locked it in the back closet whenever there was an event. A wedding, a small concert, a reading, a memorial. The room had hardwood floors that were old and crooked, holes here and there that were covered with four by fours. It was drafty, though no one noticed at the livelier events, and the walls were bumpy and patched. But the place had character, and so it was popular. The bumpy walls were painted a rich, deep mustard yellow, and the pitted floors always shone with wax, the wood colored with age; the ceiling was high and vaulted, old wooden beams running the length of the room in the old New England barn style. This was, after all, Clickstone, Vermont, home of Clickstone College, where such a place could flourish.

The man's name was Nickel. Joseph Nickel. He also owned the dairy farm up the road, or his brother did (Joe still thought of himself as part owner, having grown up there), and he worked it in the summertime. Milking cows, mixing cream and then ice cream, mashing chocolate chips and nuts and m&m's into the scoops at the customers' request. Mix-in's, they were called, for an additional fifty cents. People drove up at dusk in their cars, windows rolled down, children running and the dog barking in the back seat. Joe served them from behind a little sliding screen that was supposed to keep the mosquitoes at bay, his hands sticky with sugar and cream—and covered in mosquito bites by closing time.

In this way, many years passed. Joe pulled his mattress in and out of the Gold Dust Room. He stood in the back to watch the memorials, the acoustic guitar players, the small weddings, the poetry readings, the modern dance performance, and even, one time, a dog wedding between an Airedale and a German Shepherd.

He stood outside smoking cigarettes until everyone was gone.

He walked into town and read books at TJ's Coffeehouse, which served strong coffee and good cinnamon buns (lots of sugar, never stale). He walked the Y Trail, zig-zagging all the way up just so he could stand for a few moments at the top, gazing down at all of Clickstone below him, the houses lined with deciduous trees near the university, the straight roads criss-crossing to the intersections, the streetlights blinking red and green and yellow, the streetlamps blinking on all at once, just after dusk.

He served the families and the beaming couples and the fighting friends and the carefree teens all summer long, hands sticky.

Until, one day, he was thirty-nine. On the brink of one more decade, his last he presumed. He'd been told his fortune at the Clickstone Fair when he was seventeen. She said he would die at forty-six. She told Allen Walker that he would have three sons, and he did. She told Naomi that she would make it big on Broadway in New York (such a long shot), and she did, starring in *Goodnight, Elroy* for the last three years. She told Joe's own mother that she would find a lump in her right breast, and she did, just in time to save herself. And so. Joe prepared.

Mince and Norman were on Highway 108, driving north from Clickstone. They wanted to go swimming at Lake Champlain, which had a sea monster. This was more than legend. There were sightings and photographs, long spiked tail winding up out of the water in black and white. Videotape of the snakelike creature (big as a dragon!) winding through the lake on a dead calm day, surface like glass—except for that rupture. Documented sightings. Recorded testimony by sane people. Mince and Norman had watched a documentary about lake monsters on PBS and the Champlain monster was included. And just last week, Joe at the Gold Dust had spent an hour (waiting out a children's play) telling them about it while they sat on a bench in the sunshine, heads leaning against the Gold Dust's brick exterior. Joe's brother had seen it once. They used to go there in the summertime when the farm was doing well. A long time ago.

And so, on a break from school, Mince and Norman decided to go. They had three whole days to drive the four hours north, camp out, and drive home again. They'd lived in Clickstone their whole lives, had known each other since forever, mothers in the hospital at the same time, giving birth just hours apart, and finally, as if giving in to destiny, they'd fallen in love this year. Mince would be eighteen. She was waiting until then to, you know, she said. Norman grinned and said he'd wait forever.

They both knew this wasn't true — forever was a long, long time — but the sentiment was kind.

So they drove north, with the sweetest of intentions: to see the Lake Champlain monster.

"The bottom is made of slate," Mince said, reading from a guidebook. She wore her favorite summer shirt, off-white with tiny green buttons down the front and a frilly neck and capped sleeves. Each detail important.

Norman had slicked his hair back. He was into greasers. Bought a used black leather jacket at the thrift store in town — Marlene's Bargenes — and tore the knees of his blue jeans.

"How deep is it?"

"Unplumbable, in the middle. No one knows."

"What if we see it? We could get famous."

"People have been seeing it since nineteen fifteen."

"Like a dinosaur."

"A snake."

"In the black depths."

Norman drove slowly, savoring every moment — this, their first big adventure. They wound up 108, through the green birches and oaks and pines, robins and chickadees and sparrows chirping in the branches, colonials and farmhouses set in clusters along the way, a white-steepled church, long white fences with horses in pastures, or black and white cows grazing, or a man on a tractor working, sun beating down on his small frame, tractor turning the dirt over, getting things ready for summer. Early planting.

Once, together, they'd seen a canary—tropical yellow and green—dart from one side of Mince's yard to the other, flitting just above their heads as they drank lemonade on the deck, sunning themselves in the last of September's warmth.

"It must have escaped," said Norman.

"I hope it survives," said Mince. "Winter's coming. I wish we could catch it and save its poor little life."

The bird flew up and then up again, two jagged rises into the air, and then disappeared behind a stand of thin white birches, gangly trunks standing side by side at the edge of the yard as if unsure of their place.

Joe went hiking that morning, the same morning that Mince and Norman set off for Lake Champlain. He hiked up Bromley Mountain, a ski resort in the wintertime, the only one with all-day sun, they boasted in their brochures, because the trails were built on the southern face. He followed one of the steepest trails, careless of his heart now that it didn't matter if he conserved energy. He had six years, after all, which he figured he might as well enjoy. Live to their fullest. He hiked the steepest trail and threw caution to the wind.

He sang this to himself in a low tune, *caution to the wind, hi ho, hi ho,* all the way up the mountain. It took only three hours, even at his slow pace.

At the top, he could not see much. Mostly the tops of the trees, a rocky cliff to the south, green cut trails zigzagging and winding down the mountain, licking paths through the trees like long serpentine tails. He found a boulder and sat down, looked at the chairlift, which did nothing now but rock a little in the wind, the chairs creaking back and forth in some kind of hammock sound. He closed his eyes.

And then he heard the strangest sound—the eerie whine of an eagle hunting for food. It was only three o'clock, the wrong hour, he thought, too early, and no eagles here—only hawks. The eagles lived in Canada.

He opened his eyes. Sat up.

A golden eagle circled above him, whining high and long, Eeee! Eeeee! Looking for something.

Joe turned around and saw a woman climbing with her little weiner dog. She set her walking stick into the ground ahead of her and pulled herself forward, hiking boots tied tight up to her ankles, bright red socks poking in slivers above.

Eeee! Eeee! Circling lower, and lower, the eagle spiraled down—and Joe realized what it was after. He called out, "Look out for your little dog!" hands cupped over his mouth. "Lady!" he screamed. "Look out!"

The woman looked over to Joe. The little dog yipped at him, ran forward—a beautiful color copper, with black eyes and long, feathered ears. And the eagle, in a swift dip, swooped low, took the dog up in its talons—the size of a human hand, Joe would tell his brother later—and rose back up into the sky again, the little dog howling in pain, the woman screaming, "Barkeley! Barkeley!" up at the sky, helpless. And turning to Joe, crying: "What do we *do*? Help me!" The only two people here, and the sky stretched above them in perfect blue. The eagle flapped slowly into the blue, away, away, farther and farther, Barkeley struggling in its talons.

Joe knew there was nothing to do, that the little dog Barkeley was someone's meal tonight. But he looked at that woman, whose blond hair was still in its perfect bouffant, curled around her face; her eyes were streaming and her hands waving in the air—she was from Boston, probably, or New York, here for the weekend, a little getaway all on her own, that dog perhaps her only friend—and he did the only thing he could think of: he ran after the eagle, heading east and downhill, heart pounding, on a fool's errand.

Mince and Norman found an old resort at the eastern end of the lake. All the buildings were whitewashed, long and low except for the main house, a white farmhouse with green shudders. This was where the meals were served and the game rooms kept—bridge and chess and, just outside on a concrete slab, shuffleboard, looking over the lake, the surface choppy with waves now, trees blowing at its shore. The buildings were arranged in a semi-circle on a perfect lawn—brownish now but still neatly trimmed, cut just before the first freeze—which sloped down to the lake.

There was no one here now, because it was too early in the season. It took longer for the world to thaw here, farther north. The windows were covered with particle board, nailed to the sides of the main house and each of the long, low guesthouses. Mince and Norman stood at the edge of the shuffleboard deck and looked out at the lake, spring wind catching their clothes.

"This is it," said Mince, "Lake Champlain."

"Let's test the water."

They walked forward in their tennis shoes, right up to the edge of the lake, where the water crested forward and sucked back over the slate—*yes, it really was slate!* Mince exclaimed when she saw it. She and Norman kneeled down on the shore and held hands, kissed lightly, took off their sweaters. Norman touched the tiny green buttons on Mince's shirt, grazed them lightly with his finger-tips. She smiled and touched his cheek.

He slipped his hand into hers and squeezed three times, their I love you code.

It had been Norman's idea to go swimming. About two hours into the drive, he said, "What if we swam? As a ceremony. A commitment ceremony to each other." He was planning something, but Mince would never know.

Mince liked the idea, said, "Yes," immediately and smiled to herself, looking out the window at all the green. So much green it could fill you up for a lifetime.

Joe ran through the trees, hip-hopping rabbitesque over rocks and roots, all the way down the mountain, following—what? a spot in the sky? A nothing by now. An eagle and a dead dog.

But he kept running, for some reason he could not discern. He thought the woman was sad somehow. He only had a few years to live. He didn't do much, these days, with his life. If he could save this dog, it would be something.

Mostly, he'd just wanted to escape her screams, that woman's sad screams, too loud and desperate, wanting her little dog back, who was soaring now over the treetops, dead.

Mince and Joe slipped into the water, two naked bodies side by side, Mince covering her breasts, Joe looking into her eyes.

He would sleep with her here. He'd thought of this not in the car, but when they'd seen the whitewashed buildings, all of them abandoned, an invitation. Something romantic in this, their finding this place. They would swim together, a marriage of sorts, and then on the lawn, or in one of those boarded up houses (of course they would find a way in, nothing is impossible), they would curl together, two warm bodies in a wind-blown world, brown grass greening outside as they found each other.

He felt Mince shiver, a long quiver that ran down the length

of her long thin arm and traveled into his like an electric current carried by their bound hands.

At his farm, Joe's brother Michael cursed Joe. Where he was on this day of all days, in calving season, his brother would like to know. He walked outside to the barn, where two cows had just calved. He'd brought them in from the pasture because they'd seemed close. Michael's daughters trailed behind him, cradling two tiny orange kittens in each of their arms. They were supposed to leave them in the house with their mother, by the refrigerator where the warm air blew from a low vent right at their furred bodies. But they couldn't resist carrying them everywhere.

Michael turned and shouted, "Take them in! Now!" He and his wife had to keep yelling at the girls like this, insisting they leave that litter alone. "They'll die," he said, "if you don't watch out."

The girls turned to each other and squealed, blonde braids spinning in the air, and then they whirled on their heels and ran into the house, screen door slamming behind them, and then the heavy wood door banging shut.

Michael cursed to himself, shook his head, kept walking. It was babies all around this month. In no time at all, his wife would have their third, a boy, Michael hoped. He loved the girls, but—just one boy, he thought, I could use just one boy, an ally. Every farm needs a boy.

He slid the barn door open and heard the low moan of Diane, the farm's oldest cow, who was about to have her last calf. A breach birth, Michael saw when he checked her. He called the Gold Dust Room one more time, looking for Joe. He waited through four dull rings and then muttered, "useless," gave up, and called Will down the road.

The woman at the top of the mountain sat on a boulder and wept. Her divorce was finalized this weekend, and she had come here as a celebration, her first vacation alone. She'd approached the top of the mountain feeling victorious. Feeling independent. Happily alone.

She bowed her head into her hands and wept.

And who was that crazy man? Careening down the mountain? For all she knew, she'd scared him away. He was never coming back. She would sit here into the night, die here alone, her own body carried off by a swarm of screaming eagles, whining in her ears as they carried her off—that eerie eeee! bouncing off the mountains in a mocking echo of her death. Wouldn't her husband love it. Ex-husband. Louis.

That crazy man's eyes at the top of the mountain—so blue they were almost translucent—and to notice them at such a time, when Barkeley was being carried off—what kind of woman?

It was an accident, Norman would insist later, when questioned. I don't know what happened. We thought we saw it, the monster, and so we swam into the lake. It was so cold, and Mince's lips turned blue, but she said we had to keep going, said she was warm from swimming. A snake's tail, slipping in and out of the water like a tongue—so beautiful, you've no idea. She said, "People used to swim in this cold water for cures."

And then she slipped away, down below, and I thought it was the monster taking her. I dove down to save her. Looked for her for half an hour, I don't know, an hour, and I couldn't find her. Kept diving, up and down, and searching.

I don't know what happened.

He wept. He wept. For two years, he wept. I don't know what happened. A broken thing, repeating, an echo over and over of his own voice screaming out over that abandoned lake, the only witness those whitewashed houses, windows covered in wood — closed eyelids — and the snake in the water, tail slipping in and out, rising to the surface and then disappearing again. He loved her, really. He'd only wanted to sleep with her. Because he loved her.

Running, Joe thought of the Gold Dust Room, the things he has known. Lives passing before him — other people's lives, none of it his own. When he hiked back down, a day later, he would learn of Mince's death, a girl he'd always known, black bob of hair and a wily red smile. A sudden, unexpected death. Her parents will never get over it. They will bow their heads, walking through town, thinking of Mince, thinking of the surface of the lake, unbroken. Of unplumbable depths.

They will hate Norman, even though they will try not to. They will hate him because he let her swim in that lake on a day too cold for swimming. Mince had no insulation. Mince was a small girl, nickname suited her. Her real name Anne-Marie Pinborough. Didn't Norman know? Didn't Norman know?

Nothing will hold up in court, because there is no evidence, of course. Not even a body found. Everything swallowed up by Lake Champlain. Just another ghost left behind to walk the grounds of the whitewashed resort.

But Joe runs through the forest knowing none of this, thinking only of the past, and wondering: What have I done, all these years? What have I done but watch? Sticky hands passing out cones. What have I done?

He reached the bottom of the mountain, a road—Route 108, an old blue pick-up crawling along—Jeff McMurphy's. Spray-painted on the back bumper in white were the words: *RIP Bernice.* Outlined in red. Done with care. His wife, Bernice.

And Joe thought: This is what I need. A life, a whole life.

He thought of the woman at the top of the mountain, a city woman with new hiking boots that had given her blisters, for sure, and red socks poking up sadly out the top. Long lean legs, gangly as a girl's.

And then Joe heard a whimper. And looked up.

Diane the cow moaned and pushed and moaned and pushed. Will brought some chains, and together, he and Joe's brother Michael pulled the calf free. Outside, dusk fell.

"Dinneeeer!" one of the girls called from the door of the house.

"Let's eat," said Michael. "Come on inside."

They walked inside together, thinking everything was fine. But Diane the cow would slip away slowly in the night, bleeding too much; Michael would fall asleep and dream heavily, straight through his three o'clock alarm, and Diane would die. They would find a surrogate for the cow the next day, and the girls would feed the calf from a bottle in the morning, to their giggling delight. They didn't see Diane's body out the back, swollen with death, waiting to be buried.

The woman at the top of the mountain began to walk down, slowly. Her heels were throbbing. She knew that when she pulled her boots off, she'd find raw skin. She didn't care. She wanted Barkeley back. Louis had never wanted to do these sorts of weekends—nature weekends, he called them. He preferred hotel suites in high rises, five-star restaurants, chartered sailing cruises in tropical climes. A

New York man through and through.

Jeanne had been thinking of moving out of New York for a while now, but Barkeley had been snatched away by a giant bird, practically a dragon. She took this as a sign. She was no country girl. Dash that romance away.

She picked her way through the trees, scratching her legs on a prickly bush. She cried, and kept walking through the darkness, finding her way down.

Norman would live in a solitary house at the edge of town (his parents would try to save him, but he'd refuse to live with them, would insist on this lonely house). He would walk to Sweeney's Grocery once a week, and then walk back home again—never inviting anyone over, never making a plan—for years—because everyone would give up on him, the story of a town crazy, who was afraid to do anything at all. Afraid his guests would die on their way to his house and it would be his fault. People in town would see him and whisper, children squealing and running away, delighted, his lover's drowning as much a legend, twenty years later, as the monster itself.

Joe thought at first that he was dreaming. A hallucination. A lonely dream. He thought of a song he'd heard at the Gold Dust Room one night—a man on a vision quest, looking for his animal. Spirit animal. He'd found a horse galloping to him in the night, through the snow—body made of particles of water and air, white mane blowing in the wind. The first thing he'd found was a sound, hoofbeats hitting ground, a snort, and last of all a whinny.

This was no spirit quest, Joe thought to himself (a weiner dog his spirit animal?), but—something. It was something finding *him*.

A little dog hanging from a telephone wire, body arched in a delicate balance, slung right over that wire like something discarded from the sky.

"Goddamn," said Joe out loud. "Can't be. Barkeley?"

Barkeley looked down, black eyes disappearing in the settling dusk. He whimpered. He seemed barely alive.

"From the jaws of death," said Joe. He slapped his leg and laughed, then looked back and forth, trying to find a way to get the little dog down. A weiner dog cast from the heavens.

A branch reached out toward the wire, maybe two feet away,

close enough for Joe to reach, he was sure. It was an old oak, solid and steady for climbing. So, Joe climbed. He did not think of his pending death, three years from now. Did not think of the ice cream cones he'd be handing out soon, for three long summer months. Did not think of the Gold Dust Room and who might be scheduled for tonight, who he was disappointing by not unlocking the door and letting them in, the room heated in preparation, his mattress tucked away. He thought, least of all, of his brother Michael, or Michael's wife (who was bearing a son, they would all learn in two weeks), or the two little girls with the orange kittens or the cow Diane whom he might have helped deliver her last calf ever, if he weren't here — on this road, in the nighttime, saving a copper-colored weiner dog who'd been captured and released from an eagle.

And so he climbed the tree, and reached forward. Barkeley hardly seemed to notice him. He simply hung there, still. Joe worried he might be dead, but then the little dog wagged his tail the tiniest bit — swag swag back and forth — and let out a sigh.

Not dead.

He crawled the length of the branch that reached toward the little dog, eking his way to the end, little by little, hanging on tight, ten feet above the ground. The little dog didn't move now, waiting, it seemed, to be saved. Joe hoped he wouldn't electrocute himself. He hoped he wouldn't accidentally sling the dog down to the ground, killing him after all of this, after the dog had been spared an eagle death. Joe hoped he could do this, this one small thing in his life.

He reached forward and grabbed the little dog's tail, the only thing he could grasp, and he pulled up so that the dog's head swung in a slow circle, up and around, to Joe's own head, and landed on Joe's shoulder, where Joe caught him with his other hand—the one that had been holding the branch—and Joe held tight to the little dog but lost his balance, slipping from the branch, everything happening so fast—fingers grabbing for the branch, the bark, the darkness all around him, what was up or down he could not say, and someone behind him screaming, "Heeelllooooo? Anyone? Heeeelllloooo?" The sound of a woman lost in the woods, searching her way down. The sound of himself, an echo, reverberations falling down with him, on him, over him. He fell and he fell and he fell, for years it seemed, for an eternity, until he thudded to the ground on his back, the little dog clutched in his arms, spools of amber dust rising around his body when he landed.

And then he felt breath in his face, something warm and soft against his cheek, something wet. The little dog licking. Licking and whimpering. Then headlights falling on them both, a car rounding the bend. The woman saying, "Barkeley!" and crying. And then hands touching Joe all over, and a voice he knew from somewhere—Will's voice, going home from Michael's warm kitchen dinner and the kittens mewling and the girls giggling, carrying those things on his clothes, his skin—Joe smelled all of this, and he felt the woman touch his hair and stroke it back. He was being carried. He was going home. The mustard-colored walls.

That week, he'll see Norman in town and hear the story of that same day, Norman and Mince, and he'll try to save Norman from that darkness, tell him how turnabout life can be, how he met Lucinda on the mountain. But he won't be able to talk him out of it. No one will—not his parents, not even Mince's parents, when they forgive him ten years later. Joe will watch Norman for fifteen years (because the fortune teller was wrong about his life, after all), until the day Norman disappears, too. Just one day: gone.

In the truck, Joe saw the red slivers of her socks shaking with the bumps in the road as they drove down from Bromley. He was wrapped in something warm, and from then on, it was all he'd ever know: a sweetness to his life he'd never imagined he might enjoy. It isn't fate, he thinks, You choose. To let go of what was, to grab what's new—you choose, every second, which life you get.

❅

They made a fire in commemoration of their departure. Build a
fire when you arrive, build a fire when you leave. Sway around the
fire, shout, holler, and laugh — and maybe fight, and then become
friends, and talk, and sing, and dance. Drink around the fire. Smoke
around the fire. Imbibe, imbibe, imbibe. Take in whatever the body
needs. Water. More water. And still more. When the night turns into
morning, the fire will begin to get smaller, it will shrink and become
embers, and it will soon be nothing — just smoke. As that happens, sit
closer, lean towards each other, tell stories never told anywhere else,
secrets you've been waiting to speak, in order to expunge. Let all
the secrets unravel and unroll and fall out of you, and when you are
all spent, and your skin smells of smoke and wood, then slide home
to bed, and sleep, for a very long time. Wake up and shower. Your
body is clean. Open your eyes. Open them very wide.

❅   ❅   ❅

Acknowledgments

I'm grateful for the friends and family who helped bring this book to life. To Amy Brown and Joan Maki, faithful friends who gave me early feedback on this, and much more. Jericho Brown, Talvikki Ansel, Padma Venkatraman, David McGlynn, Matthew Lansburgh, Brian & Jenn Scheck-Kahn, Sara Gebhardt, Anna Brecke, Nancy Caronia, the Shrontzes, Ellen Goldstein, Mike Martin, and Megan Gannon for constant encouragement and writerly-camaraderie. Visual artists Jan Johnson, Danielle Krcmar, and Candice Corby-Smith, for your laughter, inspiration, and days of making. Quilters Weeks Ringle, Bill Kerr, Rebecca Loren, and Alexis Deise, for sewing lessons and community. To Thea and Leslie for showing me the way, and to Mary for giving me a soft place to land. Heartfelt thanks to Susana Gardner, for making this project come true.

Thank you to the Vermont Studio Center for the time and space to create this manuscript; I'm especially grateful to the visual artists who were in residence with me. And to the Millay Colony, for the residency that allowed me to shape the book.

Thanks a thousand times over to Deirdre McNamer, for your sharp eye, big heart, and encouragement to "make it stranger." To Peter Covino, for your support and faith all these years. And to Linda Welters, Nedra Reynolds, Valerie Karno, Annu Matthew, and Jody Lisberger, for your feedback, support, and mentorship.

As always, great big thanks to all of the Mays, and to the Primeaus and Moores—forever thank you and love.

Rachel May's first book, *Quilting with a Modern Slant*, was published by Storey/ Workman, named a Best Book of 2014 by *Library Journal* and Amazon.com, and favorably reviewed in *The Chicago Tribune*, *The LA Times*, *The Providence Journal*, and *Publisher's Weekly*. Her novel, *The Benedictines*, is forthcoming from Braddock Avenue Books. Her writing has recently appeared in *The Volta, 1913: A Journal of Forms, New Delta Review, Michigan Quarterly Review, Cream City Review, Indiana Review, Sleepingfish, Word for/Word, The Literary Review, EOAGH,* and other journals.

DUSIE

www.ingramcontent.com/pod-product-compliance
Lightning Source LLC
Chambersburg PA
CBHW051003050726
47592CB00007B/2682